# SURPRISE VIEW

## POEMS ABOUT OTLEY

Edited by Peter R White
with assistance from Sandra Burnett and John Hepworth

Published by Otley Word Feast Press, 2015
OWF Press Community Interest Company
9B Westgate, Otley, West Yorkshire LS21 3AT

www.owfpress.com

Cover design: Jane Kite

Photograph 'Cross Fragment' (p24): Genevra Kornbluth
Cover photograph and all other photographs: John Hepworth.
Thanks also to Mounseys Stationers for permission to include the photograph of their photocopier.

Thanks to Rosalind Fairclough Proofreading Services

ISBN 978-0-9934275-3-4

Printed by
imprintdigital.com, Seychelles Farm, Upton Pyne, Devon EX5 5YX
info@imprintdigital.com

# Contents

i

# V E R B E I A;

## O R,

# W H A R F D A L E,

## A   P O E M,

## DESCRIPTIVE and DIDACTIC,

### W I T H

## HISTORICAL REMARKS.

*Laudabunt alii claram Rhodon aut Mitylenen.*     H o r.

By ~~~~~~

---

"" Let other Poets in immortal lays
"" Illustrious Rhodes or Mitylene praise""—
In thee, dear Vale, companion of my birth,
I view with wond'ring eyes concenter'd Earth.
Hence we essay along VERBEIA's spring,
In humble Strain adapted verse to sing.

---

PRINTED AT YORK,

BY W. BLANCHARD AND CO. AND SOLD BY THE BOOKSELLERS THERE; BY R. WHITE,
FLEET-STREET, AND J. WALTER, CHARING-CROSS, LONDON.  A. D. 1782.

Verbeia (1782)

## Foreword

This collection has been gathered through an open invitation to submit poems about Otley. We had a huge response and couldn't include them all, but we are sure you will be delighted and entertained as well as provided with some thoughtful moments by the poems you find here.

Poems and poets aren't new to this bit of Wharfedale. In 1694 Mary Masters was born in Otley and by 1733 had written enough to swell her *Poems On Several Occasions* to over 250 pages. She is acknowledged by Thomas Maude in a footnote to his own larger-format 1782 volume *Verbeia; or, Wharfdale, a Poem*. A history of writing leading down to our own time would be interesting to trace.

And poetry thrives in the town today. Otley Poets has been meeting for more than 15 years alongside several other poetry groups and writers' groups that include successful poets. Otley's strong folk music tradition provides the town's pubs and clubs with talented singer/songwriters. Otley and its environs continue to inspire poets and poetry.

Do enjoy these poems!

Bill Fitzsimons

**Trumpet minor**

'Historic Market Town' the sign proclaims.
Civic pride, or delusional grandeur?
Perhaps a little of both – a small town
in the lee of a metropolis. It can
be forgiven for blowing its own trumpet,
a tiny ta-ra at odds with the main score.

Jo Peters
**Goddess**

Driving, I caught a glimpse
of Botticelli's Venus
wearing blue jeans
walking over Otley Bridge
where the swift Wharfe
had swirled her ashore.

She knows the mill girl
who dawdles by the forge
as the muscled smith
leans his back against
a massive flank to tip
up the feathered fetlock.

She smiles at the lad
herding his flustered sheep
across the bridge,
who will take his thirst
to the barmaid at the Black Bull
when the selling is done.

She sees the nursemaid
in Tittybottle Park turn,
push her charge up the hill
to New Hall where
the gardener's boy once
threw her a rose.

The goddess steps
aside as the young folk,
now uniformed, homework
downloaded, throng up
to Prince Henry's School where
the desire lines of courtship abide.

The invisible wind strews no roses,
but it whips her hair,
her glorious corn-coloured hair
that lifts, streams away
from the perfection
of her oval tilted face.

Howard Benn

**The Knotties Stone**

Engraved am I with the mark of man,
the symbols indiscernible, their meaning lost,
wiped clean by wind and rain,
as down below,
the Wharfe has wound and cut
its way through ancient rock
and seen small Otta Leah grow
from Saxon times to civil wars,
when thousands slew thousands;
then I knew
to keep my eyes to heaven,
where the milky stars rotate
and prophesise; pristine, and never branded
with the mark of man.

Kevin Collier

**Surprise View**

Through the haze of mid-December time, I stand here looking down
from my elevated status to the south of Otley town.
I've been here for many centuries, I've seen them come and go
and there's nowt concerning people that I haven't come to know;
folk who bridged the wily river, built the hovels, hedged the land
to the merchants and inventors and the Godly and the Grand.
As the paths grew into highways and the railway came and went,
I've seen ev'ry kiss and skirmish, and each major world event;
clans who've stayed for generations, or dropped in and never gone,
to the kids who see her bound'ries as a prison and move on.
And the ghosts of those departed walk her passageways and streets
while she alters and she stays the same and history repeats.
Now they're setting up the stalls again, there's magic in the air:
*Floreat Victoriana* and the yearly Christmas Fayre.
And it's good to see my people paying homage to the past
as they re-create the olden times, and hope the Fayre will last.
For that world was so much simpler, and its passing's seen as sad,
and they celebrate a Golden Age when things weren't Quite So Bad.
But remember as you're dressing up and quaffing spicy ale:
these'll be The Good Old Days once mind and body start to fail.
So look at what you need to change, and what you'll need to save
so that future generations thrive when you are in your grave.
And when I gaze upon the town a hundred years away
I'll see people looking back with pride at Otley's present day.

Sue Stanwell

**Moving to Otley**

Today is dank with dripping fog.
It's time to go and walk the dog.
I'll probably slip and fall in a bog
and my wellies are leaking too.

I hated the North, too cold and too grey,
it wasn't a place I intended to stay.
The gas central heating man came yesterday
he said, 'Ee you've a cracking view.'

I walk down the road – it's not going to rain,
two ponies are clopping their way up the lane,
the children are out playing conkers again
and I like it here – really I do.

Ruth Wynne

**Seek a quiet place**

Go and seek a quiet place,
feel the wind's breath,
the sun's gentle warmth
through the trees and watch
the river's waters tumble
over the weir.

Share the history of a site
in continuous use since
before the Normans; the memory
of Charles Wesley, commemorated
by a blue plaque; the navvies
who built the Bramhope Tunnel,
worshipping in the way of their forefathers,
though a long way from home.

Climb the outdoor steps
to the 'Way', with views of the river
and places where, in earlier times,
sanctuary was sought.
Some find their haven
in church, or in hearth and home;
others in solitary communion with nature.

Go and seek that quiet place –
you will surely find it in Otley.

Otley Iron

Colin Speakman

**Under Chevin side**

Under Chevin side, where Dales meet Vale
and sacred river meanders to the plain,
Pennines end. From here, hillside becks fed
ancient farms; peddlers' ways coalesced
at bridge and market to meet, talk, trade.
The turnpike road from York brought
lumbering corn wagons, elegant carriages;
whilst the river, strong and slow, turned wheels
to power rattling looms, lift forge hammers.
Came the railway's coal, that fed the boilers,
the machines to make an empire wake.
Otley was England.
                        But now, industry gone,
husks of mills are offices, restaurants, dwellings,
the town a different place – stone cobbled yards,
chapels, taverns, mere escutcheons of lives
long outlived. Tarmac, a by-pass carries traffic,
incessant, to the city close by; overhead a jet roars,
curves through the sky to a distant south.

Yet high on Chevin, the wind still rustles through
heather, bilberry, bracken, hanging slopes of oak,
beech, ash; from the summit ridge a walker's gaze
crosses two dales, to distant moors and Minster.
To the east, colossal crags inspired a vision,
Hannibal crossing Alps in snow and storm.

Sandra Burnett

**The Otley Phlox**

In his greenhouses on Pool Road,
ex-poultry man, Fred Simpson,
bred a regal strain of phlox.

Balmoral and Windsor were lauded,
along with varieties now lost,
as they dazzled in posh gardens
or rail-side allotments.

So raise your glass to Fred and his queens
of summer borders and give a cheer when you see
his Otley Choice or Otley Purple.

*Information on Fred Simpson and The Otley Phlox can be found at*
*www.otleyinbloom.co.uk/blog/otley-has-its-own-phlox/*

Rebecca M Hodel-Jones

**Otley for drivers**

Otley is a halt at traffic lights to the casual traveller and a curious gaze into hardware stores.

Otley is a consideration of whether that hard yard brush would assist me in home management.

Otley is a pondering about car parking and a potential foray deeper into those cornucopias for the house-proud.

Otley entices with pubs of character, eateries, takeaways and narrow pavements by the road, making contact with the resident pedestrians always immanent; a hand shake with car bonnet.

Otley is a pause on the journey, a time for reflection, then a change of lights, an insistent moving on pressed by the car behind, a tug away to motor on, yet refreshed by reverie.

Vernon Scannell

**An ordinary morning**

An ordinary morning in an ordinary summer
of frugal spells of sunshine and a cool
and cautionary breeze saw an old man wait,
thoughtful, on the pavement at the busy corner
where North Parade and Pool Road meet.

A car slowed obediently, then came to a halt
at the paste gems of the traffic lights. He saw at the wheel
a dark-haired young woman; on the rear seat knelt
a boy who gazed out of the window at him
with a stare that showed nothing of whatever he felt.

The woman then turned her head to inspect him
with no more concern than was shown by her son.
Her face was quite pretty but niggling anxieties,
at which he could only guess, had only begun
to pencil faint comments around her mouth and eyes.

Those eyes that were seeing, if anything there,
an ordinary old man whose life was now over;
no flicker of interest showed in her face.
How could she know he would soon walk towards
the day's white page of illimitable choice?

Jane Kite

**Early Sunday morning on Leeds Road**

Today, no stone-heavy lorries from the quarry
shake the foundations and all the white vans
are maybe keeping the Sabbath or something.

No rubber-rush or fumes yet, no crying
of trucked animals, double-deckered, waiting
in trailers for unloading at the Auction Mart.

Instead, fluorescent signs are up for the car-boot.
Its flock of customers will park higgledy-piggledy
and trail their bargains proud through the streets.

In town, purveyors of exotic meats – heat-sealed
in plastic – and pies and honey, herbs and churned
butter will be unloading for the farmers' market.

Catkins shine. The first X84 hasn't set off yet.
The old blackbird on the fence is singing.

Bill Fitzsimons

**Under the veil**

Daybreak in Otley,
and thin sunlight streams
through half-open curtains,
striping my bed with pale gold.

All is still:
not a breath of wind stirs
the air, the dawn chorus
not yet awake.

Silence is loud
on this peaceful Sunday morning –
hard to believe that elsewhere
there is grief, pain and conflict.

But what do I know
of life in Birdcage Walk
or Mount Pisgah –

what dark secrets are scratching
at cellar doors, what demons
wait to be released?

Suzanne McArdle

**Otley walk**

It was that slippery time of year
between Christmas and the New,
days slithering through our fingers
like gift ribbon.

We drove north from the city,
parked near that chippy
and slither-walked
across the town's fine bridge.

I felt bad we'd brought nothing
for the swans and ducks, as we passed
into the park, and paused
by muddied exercise equipment.

I gripped handles, placed feet;
the machine took over,
rotating legs, tugging hands,
tree branches patterned the sky,

and then I was racing back
to another Christmas,
a stringed puppet emerging
from his box, a tangle
of dark threads from arms and legs.

Jeremy Pritlove

**Walkers are welcome**

The whole town was walking.
The pubs were out first,
with a swaying gait,
slipping on puddles,
singing hoarsely as they went.
Then came the butchers,
cleavers at the ready,
welcoming other walkers
with fine cuts.
After them the stationers
carrying reams and postcards.
Clergy, children, aunts and uncles too.
Through every place where boots could go
they went.
There was not a wheel in sight:
it might not have been invented.
So all there was to hear
was the solid tramp of feet, the swish of anoraks,
the jangle of rucksacks heaving down the streets,
the pedestrian welcome of the town.

Linda Marshall

**Hey big spenders**

Lady Thrift descends on Otley
looking for bling,
steps into unfolding streets,
as one shop gives way
to another,
takes a mouthful of tea
tasting of porcelain and silver,
studies the ring
in the jeweller's window,
as if she can't part with a fortune.

Lady Spent is exhausted,
waiting for the X84
back to Skipton,
struggles with seven bags,
*Wild Thing*, *Odonata*,
*The Silk Sisters*, etc.,
after lunch at *The Pink Teapot*.
She's loaded with gifts,
glittery scarves and clothes,
whilst Lady Thrift
breezes past in a white cab,
pretending she owns the town,
and needs to buy nothing.

Peter R White

**Ale an' pork pies**

In Otley there's lots o' real ales to be 'ad –
an' some proper pork pies an' all.
An' tha can't pretend to know what's what
till tha's been there an' tried 'em all.

Start at *Weegmann's*, by 'lights, across from '*Black 'Orse*,
an' stroll by '*Black Bull* down to *Middlemiss & Son*;
then round into Boroughgate, almost opposite '*Bay 'Orse*
for a third pie, from *J.B. Wilkinson*.

You could wander right down by 'river to eat,
among 'black-'eads, pigeons and ducks,
or just 'ang about 'town an' find somewhere to sit –
'market shelter, or that bench by *Just Books*.

In much 'same way as tha can't really say
if it's best to sup gold ale, pale ale or bitter
to wash down a pie, it's a matter o' taste
as to what in a pie makes it wusser or better.

'Appen it's 'crust – made from 'ot water pastry –
d'you like one that's flaky, or one that won't sag
as it soaks up all 'jelly? An' d'you like 'gravy
all warm, an' topped up before 'pie goes in 'bag?

And what about 'meat – well cured? bright red?
succulent? lightly spiced? peppery? – or not?
Can you sense in its texture 'presence o' bread?
a bit o' gristle, mebbe? a slight 'int o' fat?

An' if *Wilkinson's* sell out (as they of'en do),
if tha's lucky, *'Old Cock* might still 'ave one to spare –
with a knife, paper napkin, a dribble o' sauce.
(An' it's 'andy, 'cos 'bus station's just over there.)

On 'way 'ome, do a little comparison test –
'ow they've combined all 'pastry, 'gravy an' 'meat.
Is peppery better or worse? – even 'best?
What the 'eck – better test 'em again, next week.

Steph Shields

**An Auction Mart incident**

Lot 69. You couldn't be there.
You left a bid, thought it quite fair,
reasonable in truth –
for a bundle of stock netting,
plus a roll of barbed wire.
Best stay away should the bidding climb higher.
You hate to drop out, you're tight-wired to win.
Then came the call to come and collect:
it's knocked down to you, so settle your bill.
Over the moor, and down the hill.

When you came home you seemed – evasive.
It's a matter of perspective, you said.
Turn it on its head, see it this way –
not what we ordered, we'll laugh one day.
Lot 96, a door stop in metal,
a hand-painted squirrel.

You what?
You paid nine quid for that?
You twot.

Mark Connors

**Prime mover**

His dad ran a stall on Otley Market
so Dave came to school each day
with his Gola bag jam-packed with pop,
crisps, mini cookies, grey chocolate bars
and an array of spice to grace any penny tray.
He gave the tuck shop a run for its money,
offered competitive credit terms,
low interest rates, discounts on birthdays
with the appropriate certificate.
There was even talk of a Christmas club;
you could bet your selection box Dave wouldn't go bust.
No one ever called him *Ginge*, nor bit his freckled hands.
Some say he invented buy-one-get-one-free;
some say he got rich ignoring sell-by dates.

John Hepworth

**The Mounsey calypso**

Mounsey's photocopier's an office model,
so only wisdom close to the word of God'll
get you safely through this tricky procedure
and that's the knowledge we'll now feed you –
it's the way we're gonna lead you.

Please read these instructions
<u>before</u> asking for <u>help</u> :

One – Lift lid where it says <u>lift.</u>

Two – Place an original (yours) face down on left
like this [ Little diagram of upright oblong ]
not [ Little diagram of crossed-through longwise oblong ]
this way.

Three – If grey panel is not lit
press button **'A'** at front on right.

Four – Make sure quantity says
**'1'** (to start with).

Five – Press green button … and
your copy is here!
Not by your left elbow? Not by my right knee?
No – somewhere just in between.
Oh praise the Lord, your copy is here!
Be overjoyed, your copy is here!
Not by your right elbow, not by your left knee,
but somewhere just in between.

No need to cry. You're home and dry. The reason why?
You've climbed the heights of Mount Seysfotercopia.
Tell your friends how your adventure ends :
You couldn't be happier than at Mount Seysfotercopia.
O yes please go now and tell every one of your friends
the way your famous brave expedition ends:
you really just could not have anything even the smallest bit
    happier
than your time with Mounsey's photocopier.

**Anglo Saxon cross fragment from All Saints Parish Church**

Oz Hardwick

**Fragments**
*(All Saints Parish Church, Otley)*


Trapped in twists and tendrils,
wound tight in limestone loops,
a faceless rider races,
reckless, on a broken beast.

Above, a worn bird
steals hard, dry fruit
from the hard, dry vine,
its beak scything darkness.

Hallowed evangelists hold
the eyes of all who pass.
*Behold this bird*, they say,
*look to this fleeing sinner*.

But time has tangled their tongues,
and their lessons, like stones, are lost.

**Mistress Dunn**

Pam Scobie

**A walk in Otley churchyard**

Sweet Mistress Dunn sleeps under snow.
Her nose was gone long years ago.
The hands once folded on her breast
now neatly severed at the wrist.
Calm as a doll, with fast-shut eyes,
in robes time-nibbled, here she lies,
a little less than human size.

No figures else within this wall.
Crosses and headstones tilt or sprawl
untended; but through hail and sun
they come to visit Annie Dunn.
And in the spring and summer time,
through grass and burdock, children climb
to lay a rough-tied daisy wreath,
and think not of the bones beneath.

Boltini

**Another offcummed-un with fancy ideas**

Any day of the week, first thing,
you might wake up to the sound of rumbling,
but don't worry:

it isn't tanks or armoured vehicles
crushing the rubble of Otley, no,
it is but the domestic thunder of our wheelie-bins
hopping off pavements, skipping over old stone setts,
as they're dragged away to the wagon,

so if you don't have to get up early
you can just roll over and go back to sleep;
quite comforting really, no climate of fear in Otley.

Not much shouting and bawling either, in Otley.
A headstrong stirk got loose at the auction;
a lollopy red-setter pup goes chasing gulls
to the perilous edge of the river in flood
boiling over the weir.

(Any bad language up our way – sorry, it's me.
Not often, but if the bathroom window's open
and somebody's pinched the special scissors
I use to trim my beard. *They've bloody well
gone. Again!* It drives me nuts.

Or if somebody parks up at the other side
of the privet hedge playing Abba. Abba! I ask you,
*Mamma Mia* blaring out. Well they can eff off.

Or if I'm trying to write and there's a deadline looming
– and there is: for this poem, damn and blast it,
midnight tonight.)

We've no chemical weapons in Otley,
we all rub along very nicely, our mettle untested.

But what if – heaven forefend – some terrible pestilence
should strike a historic spa-town up-stream
so rafts of their contagious dead and dying
come floating down to Otley? What then?

Would we give them burial or succour?
Or fend off those rafts with scaffolding poles saying,
'We don't want you here. Piss off!
Take your chance over the weir.'

Then we'd know how much had sunk in
from that symbol we erect each Easter on the Chevin.

Simon Currie

## O little town not Bethlehem

Our town, *Otley*, is *little*, both words said with no 't':
the lad, new home from primary school, was adamant.
It lies under a long ridge called *The Chevin*, pronounced
as in *shit*, not as in *church*, he assured us. I was unsure
whether he had got this from his form teacher
or from other boys. At Easter the Chevin has a cross on it
at the base of which dogs go. To shit, not to church.

The Chevin, as in shit, means most of Otley, with no 't',
gets no sun either, from November to March.
And in Otley, there's no tea to drink.
At least there wasn't till Waitrose, a 't' in the middle,
began to offer a free cuppa for those with a card.
Though, because it's free, the queue now makes it
not worth the bother. Even when free.

Otley, with no 't' or tea, does have eleven charity shops,
one of which used to be Dobson's Confectioners,
the only thing that made me as a kid sit for ninety minutes
of rugby on a Saturday afternoon, at Otley's Rugby Union
Football (no 't') Club. A reward for the way home,
Dad would buy us a mixed selection of bars
but never more than one Crunchie. Which meant war.

Joanna Sedgwick

**The Wharfe**

This is the place
we used to walk
  here
by the Wharfe
on this side
where brambles caught us
with their little hooks
and the meadowsweet's perfume
could suffocate
  here
in this place
before they put up railings
and a sign
THE RIVER IS DANGEROUS
KEEP OUT
back in a time
when we heard a troll
  no
a tannoy from the mill
  yes
a troll
squatting in a nook
under the bridge
talking to himself
and sometimes
we heard him crying
  no
the black-headed gulls screeching
  yes
we heard him crying

Maria Stephenson

**Love is not a possession**

Unclasping your fist from around the lock,
you'll turn from me,
taking back your kiss
as you fish the key from the riverbed,
guide its return to the keyhole,
gently twisting until release.
Then, you'll uncarve the initial which curls
into the ornate letter beside it.
You'll pass it to me
and retract your comments
that liken us to swans
beneath the bridge.

They don't use an ugly padlock
to assert their love.

Ian Harker

**Letting**

A week after Mum died
Grandma took me to Otley
to skim stones – something about anger.
I worked my way upstream
looking for fossils, smoothed glass,
seams of crystal – anything lasting.
Came back with an armful of stones
and a thick black leech
hanging from my ankle like a tongue.
There was blood in my footprints.
The bite went surprisingly deep.
But I didn't feel anything.

Simon Currie

**Arrested**

An affray: drunk, a lad
gains Otley Town Bridge.
Police on his heels,
he jumps over the side.

Beams criss-cross the spate,
pick up a head, once, twice.
No time for *Anything you say
may be taken down…*

Taken down over the weir
by Garnetts. The river's pomp
sweeps him, eddies and torrents,
past Pool village.

Helicopters, dressed in
the black and yellow of wasps,
relish the practice, buzz up
and down day after day.

But it's a farmer who finds him,
three weeks later. Harewood Bridge,
shackled by ripped-off branches,
spreadeagled: Leonardo's man,
naked but spun arse over tip.

Pam Scobie

**Evensong**

I've had a few lows and one or two highs,
and mostly it's been a lark.
But as for winning the Nobel Prize –
the outlook's pretty stark.

Too late for a statue cast in bronze,
but before I go into the dark,
I just want to sit here and look at swans
in Tittybottle Park.

Vernon Scannell

**The Yorkshire Dandy**

On Friday night you might observe him,
    a man of uncertain years
dressed in reactionary clothing
    who nevertheless appears
to display a certain elegance
    that you do not often see
at any time in the centre of
    Otley and most certainly
not at 10pm in Boroughgate
    where already evidence
of an over-indulged appetite
    for a superabundance
of Tetley's bitter and fish and chips
    may be detected upon
the pavement where he carefully steps
    as he, too is eating from –
not polystyrene or The Bradford
    Telegraph and Argus – but
The Times Literary Supplement
    and his hot supper is not
fishcake, cod, haddock, or even plaice,
    but sole meunière with what
else but frites and his belly contains
    a chilled Chardonnay and not
ten pints of Tetley's or John Smith's,
    nor does he bellow randy
needs to deaf skies or, alfresco, piss,
    for he is the Yorkshire Dandy.

Ruth Wynne

**The Green Man**
*(Jack o' the Green)*


Before Romans marched the ways
Jack danced beneath the ridge
bringing crops to the fertile valley.

Roused from his winter sleep, he watched
the sun rise in the east, bringing
warmth and prosperity to Otley.

He pranced and danced from May to Autumn,
guarding the harvest, chasing hogs from the strips,
to snuffle and forage in coppiced woods.

Jack saw millstones quarried on the hill,
carried down to the river's flow,
the latest harvest to grind.

He scampered free across ploughland,
oversaw cattle at the summer crossing
when waters were low and grazing green.

Returning with the bracken harvest, Jack
relaxed back into the earth to rejuvenate
and replenish the land for the coming year.

The Green Man may have lost his standing
in Kirkgate, but keep watch, you still may see him
capering around the maypole.



*The Green Man was a pub in Kirkgate in the 19th Century*

Brenda Cromwell

**The eve of Marston Moor**
*(The slightly less than true version)*


In the year of 1644,
when King and Roundheads were at war,
Cromwell said, 'I'm sorry, men,
you'll have to go up north again.
I know you think that England's crap
anywhere north of Watford Gap,
But Fairfax knows a place so fair
you'll want a caravan up there!'

So off they went, all cock-a-hoop
singing 'Ten Green Bottles' on a loop.
Now Fairfax, being a local lad,
Said, 'Ey up, men, I bet tha's glad
to reach this tiny part of 'eaven
and camp up 'ere on Otley Chevin.
So why not give thissens a treat?
Tha might be dead tomorra neet.

'Cause, if tha didn't know afore,
tha's fighting t'King at Marston Moor.
There's an inn down yonder called t'Black Bull
wi t'finest ale this side of 'Ull.
They don't 'ave Pimms or ploughman's lunch,
but that ale really packs a punch.
Don't womanise or do owt sinful,
I know thee when tha's 'ad a skin full.

At ten o'clock, be back for bed,
we've 'ell of a long day ahead.'
Those soldiers, no word of a lie,
between them, drank the cellar dry!
The locals wanted to complain,
and tell them not to come again,
but, who can blame them, they were wary,
pikestaffs and muskets can be scary.

But that ale, come to think of it,
must have made them fighting fit,
for Cromwell's men, steadfast and sure,
*won* the battle of Marston Moor.
Since then the locals, quick to learn,
have built a pub at every turn,
but I wonder if some now resent
their part in building Parliament!

Jeremy Pritlove

**Chevin**

Then the Chevin spoke:
'I am the guardian of this little town at my feet.
With my forest-thick flanks I protect it,
I breathe a cloud over Wharfedale for its comfort.
I look far to the north to ensure its safety.
My golden hoard of secrets
is older than the stars.
No hero now will come to disturb them.

I will be here still when the little town is gone,
and earth again is quiet,
as it was when I first came.'

Ian Clarke

**Seasons**

Leaving dusk starved to a bark
and passing the river's night-swim of shadow
cooling from low hills,
I dash through the night,
my shadow darting a blizzard of wings.

And below the Chevin,
pet squares of wheat,
oilseed rape sears
and a crow scars the yellow.
And after the glut,

slow writhing smoke
and the river's oily flame
laced with rumours of ice.
And as a grey wind blackens,
winter closes in,

but on the Chevin's drift of shadow
snow-bones thaw to a shiver of cotton-grass,
to a boy freewheeling,
star-shaped and summer-free,
tarmac bubbling the empty miles home.

Peter Gosling

**Bar House down**

Cresting round the great green slice of hill
the width of all the world spreads quick below
and wonder fresh replenished, here I know
I only have to look to draw my fill.
From far, near acres breathing, fallow, tilled
dark chains of oak draped loosely in a row,
with crag now scaling sharp we rumble low
to shade and softer slope and falling thrill.
Caught by burnt-loaf black, warm oated walls
we round to chime and chatter, daily things
a thread picked up, a nod, a glass set down.
Pleasures true, but still the steepside calls –
I close my eyes and see from outstretched wings
a far-thrown cloth embroidered with a town.

Judith Highcock

**From there to here**
*inspired by the Chevin*


In the shadow of the mist-shrouded rocks
the church spires reach upwards

fingers stretching from then to now
from there to here

did giants once stride across that hill
hurling rocks at the full moon

and do gods walk now across this earth
from stream to wood to field

hands moulding form out of red clay
homunculus
not Adam but Lilith
burning in the night
seeing the universe
starting to breathe

Peter R White

## Before the Chevin had trees
*(The 1st South Leeds St Peter's Scout troop, Circa 1953)*

They swarm off the dusky blue Samuel Ledgard bus,
through the gap in the dry-stone wall and up
onto the steep, craggy moorland of Otley Chevin.
Their broad-brimmed hats have pyramid crowns;
each dark green neckerchief secured by a brown
leather woggle embossed with a golden fleur-de-lis;
khaki shirts and shorts surmount knee-length socks,
green garter tabs and Cherry Blossomed boots.
They bear deadly sheath-knives on their belts
and brandish sturdy staves of coppiced ash,
scored with rings for five feet and six inches.

Knapsacks are collected in a heap, each crammed
with greaseproof-paper-parcelled sandwiches
of spam or potted meat, or even jam-and-cheese,
pop bottles refilled with super-soft water from taps in Leeds
that somehow connect to the Washburn reservoirs –
Fewston … Swinsty … Lindley Wood.

A blast on Eagle's police whistle starts The Wide Game:
they clamber over millstone grit, scurry through heather
and bilberry, lurk beneath bracken, wrestle their mates
around the rough and rocky ground, honour-bound
to concede to three taps on the head, determined
to capture the pennants of rival patrols –
white triangles emblazoned with red silhouettes
of the Peewit, Kestrel, Kingfisher, Swift.

This place was ours, that day in 1953,
when Great Alms Cliff was clearly seen,
not, as nowadays, screened by trees,
when boys could be boys into their teens
and fresh air was valued for being free.

Gail Mosley

**Menwith marchers**

I saw them on the steep road out of Otley,
straggling in file, laughing, carrying banners.
I drove past up the hill to start my walk.

Dob Park Bridge, quiet trickle of beck,
sheltering cave of sunlit leaves,
peace, mine to drink in and breathe.

Their voices alerted me,
white flash of banner through the trees,
silhouettes against the sun.

Women in a sweat of humour
clambered down to rest, settled
on mossy parapets, grass slopes.

They filled the space with ease
until a common purpose rippled through
– time to get up and leave.

I got up too and could have joined them,
remembered that my route was circular,
headed back to the place I started from.

Paul Booth

**Otley Sailing Club**

Ready about!

Not ready – can't find it!
I've seen the masts
and heard the halyards tapping in the wind
melodiously by the roadside;
but no way in, port or starboard.

OSC where are you?

Finally, after at least one 720 round Otley,
'Ship ahoy!'
Through the cattle market on a starboard tack,
up the track;
A dinghy pen.
A clubhouse.
A lake with islands,
mink,
and bonhomie.

Mandy Sutter

**Wharfe swimming**

You come here every day from work, better
you say, than a pint. It's true you're plump
in the bright brown water, as if a day on land
had dried you. You swim in a dark pool; I float
on the current's magic carpet. On the courts
toy men in cream shorts bend and straighten,
innocent of damsel flies gleaming like spilt petrol
in the reeds. Otley is seventy-five miles from
the sea. You're at my elbow, beckoning me under.
You sink, I dive. Water thuds like a trapdoor
closing. I see you in the murk, settling sideways
on stones, hair swaying in your face, inky weed.
Your breath, a mercury belch. But I'm a landlubber.
I burst back up, knowing now why your beard
is full of plankton and why a three-pronged fork
stands in our shed. And why you're sad. And why
the shower trap gets clogged with scales, weightless,
shimmering green and copper, purple and pearl.

Boltini

## Come the Revolution
*(How the Revolution began in Otley)*


stale scones
stale scones

take 'em to the bridge
take 'em to the river
take 'em to the bridge over the river

and bomb the swans
bomb the swans

hissing gaping bullyboy swans
doting on their own reflections

snooty swanky puffed-up galleons
they're big bad buggers non-egalitarian

time to be drastic
be iconoclastic

the river is for all of us
not for just the powerful that think they're gorgeous

so moorhen dabchick coot unite
get the swans do what's right

if you're out of luck
you'll hit a duck

but it's very very hard
to sink a mallard

with stale scones
rock buns

take 'em to the bridge
take 'em to the river
take 'em to the bridge over the river

and bomb the swans
bomb swans

Sandra Burnett

**Love bike**

When I tell my dad my bike's been nicked
while I delivered newspapers
to big houses on Birdcage Walk
he goes nuts, says,

*That bike was made with love,*

and reminds me of the hours he spent cobbling
it together in the Greens' draughty garage
after hard days at work.

How he grafted late into the night and his fingers
were saved from frost-bite
by Mrs Green's generous
hot toddies, and

if I hear gossips accuse him of taking advantage
while Mr Green was on night-shifts,
it's rubbish.

In my defence
I say the thief must have known my route,
the extra time it took
to push colour supplements through
snappy letterboxes.

I hold up a bleeding pinkie

but Dad goes on...
how he bartered for the frame,
hitched to Leeds to meet a mate
who'd found a Raleigh badge
and genuine Brooks saddle.

Then, he says
he needs a pint to calm his nerves
and the best we can hope for
is the brakes fail
when the thieving little sod
now riding my bike
whizzes down Otley Chevin.

He's gone before I have chance to ask,

*What brakes,* Dad

Louise Holmes

**Outpatients**

We rattled and sped
on twisty, turny roads
across the tops,
you at the wheel in your St. John's uniform
with American-tan nylons
and all-important hat,
me in my school coat
(which did for everything)
and the shiniest shoes,
polished for this holiday,
legs swinging from the too-high seat.

We drove to the farthest farms,
were offered tea
(the pace was slower then),
took people back along their bumpy tracks
past endless dry-stone walls,
your foot toying with the brake
on the long descent
to the low buildings
of Otley Hospital.
I loved the soft sound
of your chattering cargo,
the gentle vowels,
the lilting up and down
as voices rose and fell around me
like the dales we travelled.

They are building houses now
where we parked
all those years ago.
Watching the diggers change the landscape,
I can still hear your voice, 'Wait here,'
and feel again that burst of pride
when a nurse, in starched white and blue,
stopped to smile and wave at the small child
she was surprised to see
through the ambulance window.

Jo Peters

**Roads go on**

I live on a road that has recently left
a market town for the hills.
Other roads stretch up and out,
Leeds Road, Bradford Road,
they know where they are going.
But my road goes nowhere much
and has ten names in fewer miles.

Was it first trodden to come down,
down to the valley where living was easier,
or where one could sell a few sheep,
a pat of butter, a basket of peewit's eggs?

Now Bridge Street strides
over the wide river to become Billam's Hill,
named for some stout citizen.
The New Hall of Newall Carr Road
has long since crumbled,
as the road leaves the town to climb
past my house on Westroyd,
where woods were once cleared.
Now Weston Moor Road,
now Askwith Moor Road,
over bleak uplands named for villages
on the flank of the hill.
What small compasses they had!

Sourby Road remembers the farm on poor soil,
a bare living, and becomes
Rues Lane where Norse settlers cleared ancient woods,
then Cooper Lane where the barrel-maker's
son took on a moorland farm.

As the track swooped down Shepherd Hill, whose
scraggy sheep watched the Romans
make their new-fangled road across it,
now under heather and reservoir?

So I turn the road round to go back
again to the town, and feel the rumbling
cart track under the tarmac and beneath that
the narrow plodding path for hooves
or boots, below all these just the heather moor
where the unheard curlews call.

Noel Whittall

**Late bus to Leeds**

Pulped leaves on the pavements;
not quite freezing, but bloody cold.
Warm inside, windows steamed,
driver in shirtsleeves, passengers anoraked.
An obscure air of danger around:
blue lights more often *Police* than *Ambulance*.
Soon the bus is running easy and it's calm aboard,
most stops passed at speed, some cast in darkness
others on the verge of light, neon beckoning,
flickering for Christmas but lacking conviction:
still a month to go.
There are unpredicted turns,
a labyrinth of looping backroads
knits a route through Otley via Waitrose
then purl and plain round Menston station.
We crochet phrases up and down Yeadon's poets' estate.
Shakespeare Road, Ruskin Crescent, Eliot Grove.
We sway between parked roadside cars
sleeping their night away,
cholesterol to the artery of the suburbs.
Nobody talks. The late bus is a guardian of unknown thoughts.

Bruce Barnes

## John Wesley's donkey's last thoughts

*'Though I am always in haste, I am never in a hurry.' John Wesley*


Come Otley, John's spirit or the bit & snaffle,
could move me no more, the hither and thither
of his quick fire mind ceased to impress,
a donkey epithet being better suited
to my thinking – though to be fair, his aside
about 'never being in a hurry' is a burden
we have always shared. I commit my body,
that of a young ass, to His light touch.

John Hepworth

**The ballad of Wesley's revenge**

Walking round Otley by day or by night
you'd not think pedestrians at much risk of a fright –
then what a shocker awaits 'em at plain Wesley Street
if they're expecting its traffic to be equally neat.

Ah – if you're old; or, Oh – if you're young
you're never sure where the cars will come from.

If you actually live here, but you're still fairly new
and Wesley Street traffic lights make a sly grab at you,
will you not know their ways in one week or two?
No! A year will go by with no clue what they'll do.

Woah if you're old; or Oooooh if you're young
you'll never know where t'next car's coming from.

But suddenly with you for the next kerb-edge crisis:
someone living nearby since pre-decimal prices,
knowing main roads and back streets all the way through
It's *deh-durr!* caped Otley Native with words wise and true.

'Nahthen, whether tha's ancient or nobbut a young 'un
th's no way o' knowing which way 'ossless carriage is cumin'.
So - dozy or bright, old, young, settled or new,
lookaht for the peril that's looking for you.

𝔐𝔢𝔱𝔥𝔬𝔡 𝔦𝔰 t'use both sound and your sight
because we're all outshone by the Wesley Street light.
Aye, whether you're crumbling or a cool agile young 'un
tha can't be quite sure when the doom wagon's cumin'.'

Gail Mosley

**Every Friday afternoon**

Out of the city, sun in my eyes,
driving down to Otley.

Over the ring road higher sky,
King Lane, Five Ways, Golden Acre,
Brow of Black Hill Road;
viaduct trains and low-slung planes,
on the way to Otley.

Arthington, Pool, a smile at 30,
Blue Barn, 40 up to 50,
meadows and hedges along the river,
slow past gardens, square of houses,
at the edge of Otley.

Picture-frame corner, check the time,
queue in tandem, lights at red,
cut right, cut left, one way only,
Courthouse welcome, notebook open,
a pencil raised in Otley.

**Blue plaque**

Andy Robson

**Oh crikey: oh Korks**

Someone should have told us,
it ought to have been said,
informing that much sooner
that we're all officially dead.
Even though it's the same crowd
that were here the month before,
we're merely uncorked spirits –
there's a blue plaque on the door.

You've probably heard of these things,
they're always on the telly an'
there's usually the likelihood
that there's something Cromwellian.
I know we're getting on a bit
(there's no-one under twenty-four)
and we're not expected to learn it
from a blue plaque on the door.

I saw Terry at the bus station,
he just came strolling past,
and no-one's seen him in Otley
since the century before last.
So is it the demise of Otley Poets?
Can you hear this anymore?
Or are we just ghostly whispers?
There's a blue plaque on the door.

Mark Connors

**Korks Wine Bar**

*For Marjorie and Sandra*

## 1986

I felt pretty cool in my black shirt,
pink tie, chinos too long in the leg,
but a skin full soon unravelled me.
I am eyeing up any girl I can focus on.
The one I really want has grown a twin
and they both have their tongues
down some Otley psycho's throat.
I could end all this with a quiet word
in the landlady's ear:
'Every last one of us is under age!'
Clear the place, get the last bus back to Leeds
before I'm lynched.

## 2013

I think I've got the wrong night.
There's a circle of empty chairs
and no one here but me.
This feels more support group than poetry;
it might be fun pretending I've lost it all to drink.
Some strange types wander in.
A warm host welcomes us. Some bloke starts to read.
Soon, I will stand, say:
'Hi. My name is Mark. I am a poet.'

Jane Kite

**Otley poets**
*For Alan*

Begin at Birdcage Walk,
slog up Johnny Lane then the cobbled steps,
brace yourself for the hard steep climb
with rotting oak leaves underfoot,
then beech, then mixed with silver birch and larch,
to the boundary stones and steeper still
through bilberry bushes to the Chevin's top.

Look: it's spread map-like, filling the hollow,
trees on the river line, the church, small lakes,
roads, terraces, clutter of old and new,
cosseted by hills and scattered woods.

Down there are poets,

jotting, hearing accents, teasing syllables
and stresses, lines circling their minds,
beat of trochee, iamb, anapaest, rhyming
and nearly rhyming, at home, on bikes, on walks,
watching the red kites lording it, out buying vegetables,
newspapers, vodka, talking on corners,
dreaming in pubs, in the cold outside the Junction
for a smoke, or paused on stone walls.

In Otley, though you may not know it,
you're never more than a few feet from a poet.

## The Poets

**Bruce Barnes**, a Bradford-based member of Beehive Poets, writes poetry, is widely published, and would travel to Otley more often but he can't get the buses these days.

**Howard Benn**, a Leeds resident, is a freelance textile designer. He writes in his spare time, and has performed his poetry at both Headingley and Ilkley Litfests.

**Boltini** first hitch-hiked through Otley in 1968. A keen young student then, he was immediately impressed by the town's humane and flexible licensing hours. Only thirty-odd years later he was to make it his home, with fabulous consequences. Some of these can be read in *Narrow Ruled Feint with Margin* (OWF Press, 2015).

Although a resident of nearby Bradford, **Paul Booth** has had two significant encounters with Otley: he found and joined Otley Sailing Club in the early 1990s, and Otley Poets a decade later. Paul enjoys 'playing with words' – sometimes a poem emerges!

**Sandra Burnett** is an Otley poet and, although not born in Otley, claims to have lived in the town for half a century.

**Ian Clarke** was born in Wisbech, Cambridgeshire. He has been published in various magazines and anthologies including *Acumen*, *Envoi* and online with *Ink, Sweat and Tears*. Recent collections include *A Slow Stirring* (Indigo Dreams, 2012) and *BARD 132*, a broadsheet in a completely different register available from Atlantean Publishing.

**Kevin Collier** is a native of Leeds who has lived in Otley long enough for the locals to speak to him. His poems over the years have steered a course between the adolescent, the facetious, the offensive and the pretentious, often disappearing down the hole in the middle.

**Mark Connors** is a poet, novelist and award winning short fiction writer. He has had over sixty poems published in magazines and anthologies. His debut poetry pamphlet is *Life is a Long Song*, (OWF Press, 2015). His debut novel, *Stickleback*, will be published by Armley Press in 2016.

**Brenda Cromwell** lives in Burley-In-Wharfedale, and aspired to be Poet Laureate, until she realised that she had neither the talent nor the vocabulary to reach such dizzy heights. So she settled for writing silly stuff, in the hope that people would laugh with her rather than at her.

**Simon Currie** has lived in the Otley area for forty years. He has written poems more regularly the last fifteen of those. He has had a pamphlet and a collection from smith|doorstop.

**Bill Fitzsimons** is a Dublin-born local poet and is a founder member of *Lucht Focail* (Word People), an Irish writers' group. He has read at various venues in Leeds and elsewhere and has been published by *Poetry Monthly* and *Aireings*. He has also broadcast on local radio.

As a composer and occasional lyricist, **Peter Gosling** has worked on musicals, feature films and animations. He moved from London to Otley in 2014 and gets inspiration from cycling and running in the Dales.

**Oz Hardwick** is an established poet who has also published widely on medieval art and culture. He is a respected music journalist, but unfortunately suffers from occasional delusions of adequacy as a musician. To cover his tracks, he masquerades as Professor of English at Leeds Trinity University.

**Ian Harker's** work has appeared in a variety of magazines, including *The North*, *Other Poetry* and *Stand*. He was shortlisted for the Troubadour Prize in 2014, and highly commended for the Bridport Prize in 2015. His debut collection is *The End of the Sky* (Templar, 2015).

**John Hepworth** (poet, songwriter and retired Otley bookseller) tries not to be without his old Nikon Coolpix L23 for when he sees something as he's never seen it before. Poems come from he knows not where, songs from being enjoyably provoked.

A resident of Otley, **Judith Highcock** writes poetry, paints, and plays crown green bowls. The inspiration for her poems often comes from the landscape around her.

**Louise Holmes** has always had close ties with Otley. Now living a stone's-throw from the town, she says driving over the hill and seeing Wharfedale in all its glory never fails to make her day. Louise has won several poetry prizes and been published in anthologies and literary magazines.

**Rebecca M Hodel-Jones** has, for many years written poetry though has kept it squirrelled away on her hard drive. This was a bit mean so we hope you'll agree OWF have enabled her to take a step in the right sharing direction.

**Jane Kite** is an Otley Poet and one of the managing editors of Otley Word Feast Press.

**Linda Marshall** has had two collections of poetry published so far and a third might be on its way! She writes humorous verse as well, and some of her poems have been commissioned. She likes Otley for its shopping experience.

**Suzanne McArdle** writes poetry, short stories and is dipping in and out of her third novel. She has been published in various magazines and anthologies. Currently Leeds-based, she is glad that Otley is so close, since visits reminds her of the market town where she grew up.

When **Gail Mosley** retired from teaching she began writing poetry with a group at Otley Courthouse where she still goes for support and inspiration. Her work has appeared in various collections including two OWF Press anthologies and her pamphlet, *Recalculating* (OWF Press 2015).

**Jo Peters** has lived in five houses in Otley so knows all the rat runs. She also knows what a great town it is and is still amazed by all the wonderful scenery surrounding it.

**Jeremy Pritlove** sings with two groups performing early music and is a volunteer with a Leeds NHS campaign group. He enjoys walking in the Yorkshire Dales.

**Andy Robson** is mostly interested in listening to music and reading biographies of the neither rich nor famous these days. He also co-edited a poetry magazine for 43 years but that was long ago.

**Joanna Sedgwick** lives in Otley. She regularly performs her poetry at open-mic events in the area. Her poems have appeared in various anthologies and magazines, including *Magma*, *The Rialto* and *The North*. Joanna Sedgwick's first poetry pamphlet is *Travelling light*, (OWF Press, 2015).

**Vernon Scannell** (1922-2007) lived the last twenty four years of his life in North Street, Otley. During this time he published poetry, autobiographical work and a novel. He loved the town, enjoying walking his dogs on the Chevin and by the river. His favourite pub was The Red Lion.

**Pam Scobie** moved to Otley – 'a town full of rainbows' – in 2011 and plans to spend her reclining years here, writing more poems and developing her – maybe local? – hero, the poet Sid Malone: 'Private Investigator, fully licensed'.

**Maria Stephenson** is a Creative Writing Teacher and facilitates poetry workshops for the elderly. She is writing a crime novel and a poetry collection, having recently completed an MA in Creative Writing.

As a sheep farmer, **Steph Shields** is very familiar with Otley's Auction Mart. As a writer, the mart is a source of inspiration – the bidding, the buzz, the turning of small fortunes. It is a theatre. Steph is a Courthouse Writer and her short stories and poems have been published.

**Colin Speakman** is a writer and environmental campaigner living in Wharfedale who has published three slim volumes of verse.

**Sue Stanwell** moved to Otley about twenty years ago, and is still here. Now retired, she has more time for gardening, dog walking and occasional writing.

**Mandy Sutter** lives in Ilkley with her partner and a large black dog called Fable. Her latest pamphlet *Old Blue Car* (Kettlebell Press, 2015) and her novel *Stretching It* (Indigo Dreams, 2013) are available on Amazon. She's worked on 'Wharfe swimming' for years and hopes this is finally it.

**Peter R White** lives in Leeds. His poems appear in numerous anthologies including *Spokes* and *The Garden* (OWF Press, 2014). His first pamphlet is *Ways to wander* (OWF Press, 2015). Claiming poetic licence, he denies ever having consumed three pork pies in a single visit to Otley.

**Noel Whittall's** books and poetry have been translated into several languages including Finnish, Japanese and Slovenian. He wasn't always asked first and cheques rarely followed.

**Ruth Wynne,** lately of Otley, is a relative newcomer to the poetry world. She is a member of the Irish writers' group *Lucht Focail* and has read at many venues in and around Leeds.

## Acknowledgements

Boltini's 'Come the Revolution' was previously published in *Narrow Ruled Feint with Margin* (OWF Press 2015).

A version of Simon Currie's 'Arrested' was previously published in *Other Poetry* (Durham, 2005).

Kevin Collier's 'Surprise View' was previously published in one of the *Otley Christmas Fayre* programmes.

Jane Kite's 'Otley Poets' was previously published in *Workout* (Otley Poetry Gym, 2011).

Vernon Scannell's 'An Ordinary Morning' was previously published in *A Place to Live* (Happy Dragons Press 2007) and 'The Yorkshire Dandy' was published in *Views and Distances* (Enitharmon, 2000).

Noel Witthall's 'Late bus to Leeds' was previously published in *Speak Another Language* (OWF Press, 2014).